Practical Access

How To Make Your Business More Affordably Accessible

by
Frank & Dawn Yeager

LCI Media, 5204 Faulk Dr., Export, PA 15632

lanalexcloyd.com

Copyright ©2022 by Yeagers Consulting Co.

All rights reserved.

The information provided within this book is for general informational purposes only. While we try to keep the information up-to-date and correct, there are no representations or warranties, express or implied, about the completeness, accuracy, reliability, suitability, or availability with respect to the information, products, services, or related graphics contained in this eBook for any purpose. Any use of this information is at your own risk.

The information provided in this book does not, and is not intended to, constitute legal advice; instead, all information, content, and materials available on this site are for general informational purposes only. Information on this website may not constitute the most up-to-date legal or other information. Readers of this book should contact their attorney to obtain advice with respect to any particular legal matter. No reader should act or refrain from acting on the basis of information in this book without first seeking legal advice from counsel in the relevant jurisdiction. Only your individual attorney can provide assurances that the information contained herein – and your interpretation of it – is applicable or appropriate to your particular situation.

Table of Contents

Introduction 1
Is There Really a Need? 3
Definition of Practical Access 8
    Collect information 8
    Create a plan 8
    Create your budget 9
    Make things happen 10
    Collect feedback 10
Why Practical Access? 11
Myths and Misconceptions 13
Impediments to Success 15
Our Background 18
Our Reality 21
Our Inspiration 25
Getting Started 26
Top 3 Reasons to Get Started 28

Table of Contents

Roadblocks 30

The First Step 32

Pitfalls 34

Smoking the Competition 36

Saving Time 40

Biggest Mistake 42

Access Efficiency 44

Our Revelations 47

Into the Future 49

Final Thoughts 53

Yeagers Consulting 56

Introduction

Why is the topic of business accessibility so important for business owners? Just for clarity, let us define what we mean by "business owner".

Anyone who owns or leases property that constitutes a public accommodation needs to address accessibility. For instance, a person or company may own a building that houses multiple different individual enterprises. When we say "business owner", we mean both the owner of the property or lessor, as well as the proprietors of each individual enterprise or lessee. We'll use the term business owner for simplicity.

In our opinion, providing accessible spaces is just an extension of good customer service and human resources management. Let's discuss an example.

Colonial Williamsburg is far from accessible. Being a faithful recreation of a 17th century town, it was never designed to be. Small things have been done where possible to improve accessibility but there are quite a few places that a mobility-impaired person would find it difficult, if not impossible to go.

What sets them apart is their customer service. It is quite simply outstanding. Dawn was able to enjoy the majority of the town's offerings from the comfort of her wheelchair.

That's because the staff went the extra mile to make her feel welcome. Artisans brought examples of their work to her when she wasn't able to access their work spaces. Whenever humanly possible, they provided a way for her to access those areas herself.

Everywhere we went, the staff of Colonial Williamsburg made an effort to engage, educate, and entertain every single patron. It was such an amazing experience that we've returned and have plans to do so again.

Between a fifth and a quarter, so 20 to 25% of people in the United States are disabled. On top of that, over 60% of households in the United States have a disabled family member. That's a pretty big section of the population that, if you are not providing accessibility, then you are missing out on revenue from potential customers.

In this book, we'll discuss why Practical Access is so important to business owners and how to effectively implement it.

You'll learn about our background and experiences with accessibility and the many ways that business owners can get tripped up. Then we'll provide solid solutions to your business accessibility problems and concerns.

Is There Really a Need?

The Americans with Disabilities Act was passed in 1990 and, for the first time, accessibility became the law. Two decades later, the Department of Justice published an update to accessibility guidelines to address shortcomings in the existing rules.

That means it has been over 30 years since the passage of a law that mandates barrier removal from buildings utilized by the public and accessible design.

By now, all public buildings should be at least mostly accessible, right?

Dawn and I lived in an eighties double wide. Overall, accessibility wise, it wasn't perfect. It wasn't built with accessibility in mind and we knew that when we moved into it.

There were a couple of issues like, hallways and doors are narrow and stuff like that, but, overall, it is more accessible than a lot of the places of business that we've been in.

The new businesses or renovated places that, under ADA design standards, should be at least nominally accessible fall very short of the mark.

The design standards are more stringent now. So, the fact that what we've been in umpteen hotels that you couldn't move around in, we've been in umpteen restaurants that you couldn't navigate, makes facility usage as a disabled person very frustrating.

And that was in Dawn's original narrow, manual chair. We had trouble using facilities in a chair that was far more maneuverable and able to go into more restricted spaces. Now she's in a 350-pound power chair that takes significantly more space to maneuver.

Once we went into a popular steak house to have dinner with some extended family. Everything up to the point of going in the door was perfect.

Parking and access to the restaurant were spacious and clear. All the curb cuts and sidewalks were generous with very gentle slopes.

Then we went in the door.

Long story short to avoid a long rant, it seemed as though the restaurant had been designed for tables. There was almost no walking space to speak of.

The entryway was maybe 42 inches wide overall. With potential diners waiting all around, there was about 20 inches of open floor space to move a wheelchair through. Not ideal.

The aisle way between the tables was about 36 inches wide. Two able-bodied people had trouble passing in this space. With walkers and other accessories, there was about half that space to move a wheelchair through. Extremely difficult.

The spacing between the tables would have been perfect for someone the girth of Olive Oyl. Nearly everyone's chairs banged against those behind them when they sat down. God forbid you have to go to the bathroom. There was nowhere to swing for a wheelchair to get under the table. Ridiculous!

This isn't the exception. We've had multiple restaurants, mostly chains, that you couldn't get in the door and then you couldn't move once you were inside. Unless the place was empty, there was nowhere to go and the tables were too close together. Even when we were using the manual chair, I would have to literally pick Dawn up and sort of side slip her in so she could eat at the table.

This shouldn't be the rule. These are often large chain restaurants. Surprisingly, smaller establishments with smaller budgets often do a better job of accommodation.

Retail stores don't fare any better. A lot of the stores we've been in; the aisle ways were narrower. And even when they weren't, they wind up with these temporary displays stuck all over the place that you can't get around.

Shopping shouldn't be like navigating an obstacle course!

In so many stores, like in the grocery store for instance, Dawn would start down the aisle and then somebody with a cart was coming the other way. Someone would have to back out so the other could pass.

And these are often stores that had been rearranged to supposedly make it better for shoppers. And still, it's not nearly as good as it could be.

It's still lacking and there are a lot of major points where they just miss the mark.

On the good side, when somebody is doing average with accessibility, you're like, "Wow, that's great!"

It's not even a matter of price range. Many "better" restaurants if we've been in that you couldn't move in, and yet you go into, these old diners in some places and there's all kinds of room.

On top of that, they bend over backward to accommodate you. They're so much more accommodating that, if we didn't know better, we'd think they were desperate for the business.

There have been experiences that were terrific! There are restaurants that have hit it out of the park from beginning to end.

Like the small buffet we visited in a small town outside State College. We thought we were in trouble when we came down the sidewalk and saw three steps to the door.

Before we had a minute to think about it, the door swung open and the hostess stepped out. She apologized for the inconvenience and asked if we minded using the delivery entrance.

That turned out to be through the kitchen as well, which was less than ideal and we began to have second thoughts. Then we entered the dining room.

Everything was wide open! Dawn was easily able to navigate everywhere she needed to go. Getting under the table was effortless.

When the hostess saw me helping Dawn get a plate, she asked if she could help. When Dawn consented, a waitress stepped in and ushered Dawn through the selection, made sure she got everything she needed, and ushered her back to the table.

The entire experience, with one minor hiccup of the entrance, was terrific!

So the big thing is that as far as performance under the ADA, there is still a long way to go. If an eighties double wide is outperforming modern, accessible businesses, then, you know, there's definitely a problem in how it's being applied.

The application leaves a lot to be desired. Even though all of these rules are there, when you go into a place in a manual wheelchair, you can't use it, let alone in a power chair, which is higher and bigger.

In a lot of cases, it's not even major changes that need to be made. Often, changes in arrangement would be sufficient to vastly improve accessibility.

That's something to keep in mind. You don't necessarily have to make major changes and everything that you do to improve is a step forward.

Definition of Practical Access

The purpose of this book is not only to demonstrate the shortcomings of how accessibility is applied in the built environment and in the design process. We want to present a clear, simple process for addressing accessibility that encourages businesses to be proactive.

The application of accessibility leaves a lot to be desired in a lot of cases. What we advocate is what we call Practical Access. The approach can be described pretty simply.

Collect information

You have to know where you are to determine where to go. Flying by the seat of your pants is a sure way to waste money.

Start by doing an accessibility survey. This will tell you how accessible your facility is now and where it falls short.

At the same time, talk to customers, staff, and disability advocates. Find out what they need from spaces like yours. They'll be able to tell you immediately what areas are most in need of attention.

Create a plan

Once you have all the information together, get an engineer involved. They'll be able to guide you regarding the preparation needed for each project and how everything will work together.

Prioritize your projects with that guidance and estimate the cost of each step. Evaluate your budget and decide how much can be dedicated to accessibility.

Chunk everything down into the smallest steps possible. That makes budgeting easier and allows you to show constant, visible improvement.

Make sure your plan is in the form of a timeline and in written format. You also want to be careful to keep both staff and customers in mind during the planning.

Create your budget

Going forward, your accessibility plan will facilitate creating an operating budget so that funds are always set aside for improving accessibility.

Keep in mind that construction costs are going to continually increase. Only create estimates a year or two in advance and make sure they are adjusted for inflation as needed.

Something to keep in mind is the availability of grants and incentives. The federal government provides tax credits and incentives. Many state and local governments do as well.

That means your accessibility budget can go farther. If you don't use all of a credit in a given year, some tax laws, federal for sure, allow you to apply the unused portion to the cost basis of the facility and depreciated it over the life of the building.

The benefit is that you are inherently increasing the value of the building by doing good. While you create a more welcoming and usable atmosphere for customers and staff, you not only save money now but into the future.

Keep in mind that construction costs are not the only expense that can be used for credits. Engineering, consulting, and other expenses can often be included.

Make things happen

Even if you don't have enough money to complete projects right away, start setting that money aside. Having a separate fund on your books shows your intention.

Compile the construction documentation and get the engineering completed for your first project as soon as practical. When you think you're ready, put the project out for bids.

Once you have bids on the project, look them over to make sure your budget was adequate. If not, put the project on hold until the funds are available. Otherwise, move forward.

Collect feedback

Go back to the folks you surveyed initially and survey them again. Find out how they feel about your efforts and what else they'd like to see.

This will help you stay on top of the projects that are most important to them and adjust your plan, if necessary. You'll also find out other information you might not expect.

It also shows them that they are the focus of your efforts. The positive impression will pay dividends for your business.

Why Practical Access?

Our approach is methodical. It's about chunking things down and working from the outside in. The focus stays on the people accessibility serves so your efforts are effective in both cost and impact.

Staff and customer needs are integrated in every step. No one feels left out of any part of the process and you're always working on their most immediate needs.

The collaborative aspect ensures your plan's effectiveness. Customers and staff feel like they have a stake in your accessibility plan which improves your company culture and public relations.

Practical Access also provides maximum ROI for each dollar spent doing good. Tax strategies maximize your budget and allow a more aggressive plan. Affordability is just baked into the cake.

This holistic approach improves customer service, company culture, community impact, and more to help you build an inclusive brand. This perception will attract your ideal customers and staff.

By design, Practical Access helps reduce or eliminate overwhelm from the process. Business owners aren't left feeling like, "Oh my gosh, accessibility is this huge undertaking that I just can't afford, or I don't know what to do!"

That leads to taking a major risk and not doing anything. But that's not really a viable option because the ADA is the law.

You don't want to be in a position that you're forced by lawsuit to have to do it. You don't want to be reactive. You want to be proactive.

Myths and Misconceptions

There are a couple warnings for business owners about business accessibility.

There are a lot of misconceptions about how the ADA applies. For instance, we've heard business owners say that if it presents an unreasonable burden, I don't have to do accessibility projects.

No, that's not true. You don't have to do the whole thing right now. It doesn't mean that you don't have to do it at all. You need to make progress, ongoing progress toward barrier removal under the law.

You need to have a solid plan in place. Not having a plan just simply isn't an option. If you have a plan, you're actually defending yourself in the event that somebody does bring a lawsuit.

You are able to present your accessibility plan as evidence of intent. You say, "Hey, we went through the survey process, we went through everything, and we have this plan and we're making progress and this is what our plan looks like."

But the idea that, if it's too expensive, I don't have to do it. No, that's not true at all.

Not to be gloom and doom here, but more lawsuits are being brought in general. More and more people are getting out.

The last statistic we saw was that there were $300 million worth of awards in litigation last year. And that doesn't count everything. Settlements and other circumstances weren't included in that number. Overall, that's a pretty significant number.

Besides the awards, if a business is involved in litigation, there's the negative publicity to consider. The community impression is going to be negatively impacted by press stories about litigation.

No matter what you're losing, and no matter what you're spending money on attorneys and you're sitting in court. That costs money in and of itself.

That's not to say that Practical Access will prevent you from being sued. Drive-by lawsuits have become a cottage industry these days. People looking for a quick buck and their attorneys drag unsuspecting business owners into court frivolously.

However, if you're proactive, have a plan, and involve the community and your staff, lawsuits become less likely. When you are involved in one, you have a more credible case when you have a written plan and budget.

The public relations aspect of a lawsuit is less as well. When you create an inclusive brand, people are less likely to believe that kind of negative press and may even speak out against it.

Impediments to Success

How important is business accessibility business owner's success?

The Practical Access approach really is designed to be inherently cost effective because it's an outside in approach. Practical access is supposed to be practical.

So, you work on your parking areas and your approaches before you worry about bathrooms and so forth. Because if you're fixing a bathroom that nobody's using, it's kind of pointless to spend that money.

So, our methodology allows business owners to address the issues in order of importance both to their staff and to their their customers in a way that you know, it's needed at this point.

It's a step by step process work from outside in that addresses things in a certain order. That way you're presenting the most effective solution at the time that it's needed.

We can't say possibly stress enough how important accessibility is, because this, as we said in the beginning, is a large segment of the population. The good will that you're generating by being proactive about this with your customers, with the community, and staff is crucial.

To present an example, there was a store that somebody had recommended that was supposed to be this amazing store. They loved this store.

So we pull in the parking lot, we park, Frank gets Dawn out of the truck and into the wheelchair. There's an area between the parking spaces where, it's hatched out and supposed to be an approach to the entrance to the sidewalk.

There were curbs installed at the end of the spaces and Dawn's narrow, manual chair wouldn't fit in between the curbs.

There was nowhere else to get up to the sidewalk. The only way to go was out into traffic, run into oncoming traffic, and jump the curb onto the sidewalk. It was incredibly unsafe.

We finally just got back into the truck and left and never even went into the store because it was impossible. It just wasn't worth it.

People aren't going to work that hard to get into your store. Then word gets around if a place is not accessible or it's hard to get into.

If an establishment is difficult for a wheelchair, the wheelchair isn't the only one that you're excluding. Consider the mom with the child in a stroller. It could be Grandma with a walker or Uncle Fred with a cane.

There are different levels of mobility and each have different challenges. But not every barrier only affects them. Dawn's manual chair fits through a 24-inch doorway so, there's no way you're getting a walker in between them, let alone a wheelchair. Or that a mom with a stroller who is trying to keep the little ducklings together.

Again, people aren't going to work that hard to try to get inside and you've lost them as a customer because they're not coming back. There are plenty of other stores.

If you've lost them outside, it's just stupid to make an accessible bathroom whenever people can't even get in the building. So why spend money to do that?

Same thing applies to sticking an elevator in. Why bother if they can't get in a building because it's pretty pointless and it may even wind up being money totally wasted.

Our Background

What is our background with business accessibility? First off, we live it every day.

Dawn was injured in an automobile accident. She was a passenger and broke her neck two weeks after high school graduation. And without completely telling her age, that was over 30 years ago. So, she is a quadriplegic and has to use a wheelchair.

Since then, she has earned three Bachelor's Degrees and an MBA. While doing that, she pivoted from her expected career path in medicine to management and accounting including, managing a CPA office, nearly a decade with the FBI, public school treasurer, and corporate CFO.

Frank worked as a contractor for over 30 years. Starting with modifications in houses for multiple disabled people such as ramps, lifts, bathroom modifications, and that kind of thing, he progressed to businesses so that the disabled could better access them.

Then he met Dawn and experienced a real eye-opener! Even doing modifications for so long he'd never truly realized the challenges faced by the disabled. Suddenly, he got to experience it on a day to day basis.

Life became planning and improvising how to manage the basics of life to allow he and Dawn to enjoy experiences most take for granted.

Dawn appreciates finding someone who is willing and able to do all the things that enable her to enjoy life to the fullest. She has seen people without a caregiver or with one who isn't able to do the things Frank commonly does for her.

It's not just the physical things like being able to pick her up and carry her anywhere they need to. She also knows that, for some people, it simply isn't as easy.

For instance, there are people with ventilators and other devices that don't allow someone to simply scoop them out of a chair and run off with them.

Frank is grateful to have discovered an entirely new world where small barriers are a big deal. He and Dawn have dedicated their time and experience to trying to make the world more accessible for everyone.

As far as education in accessibility, Frank initially got involved in home modifications through an inquiry from an organization representing someone in a somewhat emergency situation.

In order to do things right, he had to sit down and do the research to find out how to do these modifications correctly. He dug into the regulations and rules started the work. After doing several jobs in that manner, he got certified in accessibility and stuff through, InterNACHI and CCPIA as a property inspector.

After over 30 years as a contractor plus several years as an inspector, the built environment is something that Frank is pretty familiar with in general.

For Dawn, just two weeks after high school graduation, becoming a quadriplegic, she's been living this experience for over 30 years. At the time, just being 18 and wanting to move on and go into college, she built a background is in business with undergrad degrees in accounting, business administration and management, and then an MBA.

She understands from both a personal and a business standpoint how accessibility just makes sense as a good business practice and how it affects, how it affects individuals, and the risk for businesses as well.

After 15 years of marriage, both of them got to experience a much wider world. They saw the variety of barriers that the disabled commonly had to overcome if they were able.

They realized that most of them weren't purposeful. Rather, most people lack the insight that living with disability gives you. They are striving to give everyone the ability to see more clearly and act to eliminate barrier wherever possible.

Our Reality

Our entire goal is to allow others to learn from our experiences. From designers to builders to facility owners, we want everyone to understand what real accessibility is and be able to put it into action.

Business accessibility depends on the business you're in. Just being able to recognize trouble spots instinctively allows business owners and designers to act more proactively. That comes with practice.

For example, many times we have been staying in a hotel and, when we went in, we quickly realized Dawn getting around was going to be a problem.

First off, there's often too much furniture and many times some of it is in the traffic area. There isn't enough space between the foot of the bed and a dresser.

Fortunately, in most cases when we get in a situation that is less than ideal, Frank is physically able to pick Dawn up. Or sometimes muscle things around to make it work. But not everybody is that fortunate.

Then there is often the fact that Dawn couldn't get under or even sideways in front of the sink. She would have to brush her teeth using cups as basins.

The shower presents a different set of challenges. Often, there is a tub/shower combination. We have never had a shower chair or transfer bench available to use without asking. When we get them, there are never arms on the chair so Dawn has difficulties with stability.

Of the hotels we've stayed in, two had integral shower benches and only one had a roll-in shower. The seats are always opposite the shower controls so there is no option to adjust water temperature and reach the hand shower from the bench. That means you need to do it prior to settling on the bench.

So when you hopefully get the hand shower placed somewhere that it will stay, water cheerfully spraying everywhere, then you need to transfer to the shower seat and get ahold of it without knocking onto the floor which necessitates starting the entire process all over again.

Let's also discuss the chairs and benches. We have never met anyone who has ever used them who has found them comfortable. With mobility-impaired people, these things can actually cause injury.

On two occasions, Dawn has gotten a pressure ulcer on her behind from these lovely torture devices. Say it with us, plastic and slats are bad for the bum.

Disabled people get into the habit of carrying a wide variety of equipment with them when travelling. Cushions for shower and toilet seats are one such necessity.

It's not just people in a wheelchair who struggle. The furniture situation is often hazardous for almost anyone. Sinks being located outside the bathroom are not intuitive so the blind have trouble finding them.

Restaurants present different challenges altogether. Often, it's nearly impossible to get a wheelchair inside without help. Then there are people standing there waiting and you're almost running over their toes just to get in.

Once that obstacle is navigated, getting to and under a table is difficult. If there is one walker, cane, or wheelchair in the aisle, it's impossible. That doesn't even count the hazard to staff and guests when trays of hot food are being carried.

Retail establishments really run the gamut. Some are designed to meet the letter of the ADA but that's where accessibility seems to end.

Even when aisles are adequately wide, you find a multitude of little temporary displays that stick out everywhere and are constantly in the way. Some are even hazardous because they aren't very stable and can fall on someone.

Funny story, we went to a department store and they had display tables with drapes over the tables at Christmas time. Frank went to look at something and Dawn pulled up to the display in her manual chair and looked things over.

Frank heard her calling and went over. She said, "I'm stuck." the drape trailed onto the floor and when she'd pulled up, her caster got onto the drape. And then whenever she went to back up, it swiveled and got caught.

Luckily, Dawn noticed the problem and Frank was there to fix it or the entire display might have been pulled over on top of her! That particular situation would have presented a potential hazard for anyone.

And that's where the practical part of Practical Access really comes in. It's not just the ADA accessibility, because ADA can dictate there has to be a hand shower. There has to be a shower seat for it. Okay. But is it practical to have the shower bench on one end and the controls on the other?

Is it practical to have dining tables so close together that the able-bodied struggle to sit down let alone try to get a wheelchair under them?

Can it be considered remotely practical to create hazards in aisles to anyone unfortunate enough to bump into them?

Keeping these things in mind is critical for businesses. You need to adopt a different mindset.

The disabled won't be the only ones to benefit from this change either. All your customers' experiences will be improved.

Our Inspiration

We have family members that are business owners. All the things we mention in this book are taken from our personal experiences. The combination of business knowledge and life experiences have shown that we can help a lot of people, business owners and the disabled alike.

We know that the principals of Practical Access create better outcomes for everyone. Our goal is to guide business owners and designers to look beyond the ADA requirements and see the people.

We're friends with business owners. We have family that are business that are business owners. They're not people that want to be negligent.

We've lost track of how many times have we been into a business of someone we know where they were like, "Oh my God, I didn't know! I didn't realize you couldn't (insert problem here)!"

They would literally change things immediately. Then they would make changes to their place of business based on their new insight. Business owners don't want to exclude disabled people. They often just don't realize where the problems are.

These experiences have made us realize the good we can accomplish by raising awareness and providing a clear, practical ways to accomplish accessibility.

Getting Started

A lot of getting started with accessibility is just about awareness. I don't think that anybody, business owner or otherwise, sets out to intentionally exclude anybody.

There's a lot of misconception about the ADA. There's not a ton of education about the ADA that is clear and practical.

A lot of times you only hear about the negative things like the lawsuits because that's what makes headlines.

So as far as getting started quickly, we think, is about awareness. Take a look around, look for the things that can create barriers. A lot of times it's as simple as realizing that if you can't navigate a stroller through it, you ain't getting a wheelchair through it. It's a problem that needs addressed.

Sometimes business owners don't know what they don't know. We run into this constantly. People were making an honest effort but didn't realize they were wasting money on something that didn't work.

That's an area where consultants and inspectors and so forth can help. Our company tries to be more comprehensive, but even a commercial accessibility inspector can help give you a solid starting point.

There's actually a certification out there called a Customer Access Specialist. It is an access inspector where they come in, go through, and they have a checklist that's taken directly from the ADA.

They can go through, assess your facility, and give you a report that lets you know where the shortcomings are as far as they've seen.

A lot of the success of that approach is based on the experience level of your inspector. A lot of them have varying levels of experience. But, at the minimum, getting that inspection would make you aware of more than you might be aware of otherwise.

How practical is that? Well, if you don't, like we said, you don't know what you don't know. And if you at least get somebody to come in and do a survey, whether it's a hundred percent or not, you're at least getting started.

For a few hundred dollars, you'll at least have somewhere to start which is far better than doing nothing at all.

Top 3 Reasons to Get Started

First, like we'd mentioned, you are excluding a significant demographic that has money to spend.

They want to be able to use your restaurant. They want to be able to come in and buy a cheeseburger. They want to be able to stay the night at your hotel. They want to be able to come in and shop at your store.

They want to be able to do those things, they have the money to spend, and, if they can't get in, they're going to go somewhere else where they can. So not doing it is definitely not conducive to good business.

Again, over 60% of households have at least one disabled family member, which means, if grandma can't get in your store, we're shopping somewhere else.

Eventually, you start making people angry. You foster a bad feeling that you just don't care. When people realize that your place isn't accessible and nothing ever happens to change that, it just leaves a bad taste in people's mouth.

And, secondly, just because someone is able-bodied and can get around a store that has restrictive areas that a mobility-impaired person couldn't doesn't mean they're not taking it all in to see if they can see if they could bring grandma in to go Christmas shopping or to come for a family dinner.

There have been many times have Frank has come home and said, "Hey there, I was at this really cool store, but I couldn't take you there because you wouldn't be able to get around."

Finally, the third reason that you should get started in general is because accessible spaces are just better for everybody.

This isn't going away. These requirements are not going to get easier. If anything, they're going to expand.

But when you go into a space that is truly accessible, that a mobility-impaired person can actually use with wider aisles and lower shelves and better lighting. And it's wide open. It's just an amazing experience.

It creates a more welcoming environment overall. So, just because it's accessibility doesn't necessarily mean that the disabled are the only people that it's going to appeal to. It's a better environment for everyone.

Not only is it a better experience for customers and clients. Everyone that works there has a better environment as well. Employees will definitely appreciate the accessible environment.

Roadblocks

Many business owners have misconceptions about how the ADA applies to them. Even though it's the law, it's often treated as though it's optional.

One big misconception that if it's too expensive, I don't have to do it. That's simply not true. Barrier removal is the law, period. You have to make an effort to remove barriers.

And it doesn't matter if it's a million-dollar project and you have a thousandaire budget. You don't have to spend that money this year.

But you have to start saving money and show that you're saving money for this specific project to demonstrate that you're actually making an effort toward removing those barriers. If you don't, you're in violation of, of the ADA.

You have to do it or you're rolling dice.

Which brings us to the next point. There's a misconception that these projects are all very expensive. There are actually many that are not.

Many times improving accessibility is as simple as adjusting your use of space. Simply put, more isn't always better. You want to maximize your potential income per square foot but not at the expense of your customers and staff being able to utilize the space.

It seems the biggest obstacle for business accessibility is as simple as overwhelm. They know they should do it, but they don't know where to start so they put it off until later.

The solutions to these problems can be as simple as reliable information.

The First Step

Getting started with accessibility begins with an accessibility survey. That's the best way to determine where your facility needs attention.

Who does it is less important than getting it done. You need to get it on the books. Schedule it as soon as possible.

You can call an inspector or consultant to perform the survey for you. We have created training to show how to do it yourself. Whether you hire someone else do it, have a staff member do it, or whether you do it yourself get the survey done.

That way you know where you stand from the beginning. That's the big thing. The focus of most of those things, especially for somebody doesn't have a lot of experience, is going to be the hot button things.

That will include things like, are your parking spaces the way they're supposed to be? Do you have a ramp to your door? Are they able to get in the door? Are they able to get on the ramp? Are they able to use the bathroom?

So no matter who does your survey, they're going to be checking the big hot button stuff. The basics. That gets you started.

A more experienced accessibility consultant is going to know a bit more about things like landings and turning areas and things like that. But, if you at least get started and start to develop a plan, it doesn't matter what person you use to do the survey. Getting started is half the battle.

Pitfalls

We'd be remiss not to mention the mistakes we see every day. Keeping things in mind will make a big difference in how successful you are with accessibility.

The biggest pitfall we see most often is people wasting money. It's not necessarily that the project doesn't need done. It just doesn't need done yet.

For instance, like we mentioned before, to make an accessible bathroom when people in wheelchairs can't get into the building.

Improving the employee lounge area so it's a hundred percent accessible, but there's a step to get in.

The biggest pitfall is not realizing that there is a progression. There is an order in which things need to be done. If you ignore that, you're going to spend your budget on projects that don't really have any immediate effect.

The other big pitfall would be, as we've mentioned multiple times, trying to ignore it. It's not going anywhere. It's only going to increase.

With the new prevalence of drive by lawsuits. Unfortunately, there's been a surge over the past couple of years of people using this method to make money.

They drive down the road, they look at your place of business and, if there's a visible accessibility issue, they just go ahead and file a lawsuit. There are actually attorneys who are being investigated and charged because they will take multiple frivolous cases and litigate.

Because it is the law, you can easily get caught up in this type of foolishness. If you then have problems with accessibility and no plan to address it, you can wind up becoming an unwitting victim with no way to fight it.

So it's better for businesses to be proactive. You don't want to be put in the position of being reactionary.

Smoking the Competition

This isn't usually what you think about when you're considering accessibility but hear us out. When it comes to getting a leg up on the competition, every little bit helps.

If your business is seen as an inclusive brand and has better access, isn't that a selling point? More inviting spaces and greater inclusion are going to create warm, fuzzy feelings all around.

We all know that perception is half the battle. When the public, whether that's your local community or nationwide, sees your business demonstrate care for its customers and staff, you win.

How do you do that?

Don't be afraid to reach out to an expert, whomever that may be. Whether that's us or somebody else. Find someone to guide you.

There are multiple parts to the ADA. There's a part that governs mainly government buildings. And that doesn't necessarily apply to most businesses.

There's a part that governs employment and then there's a part that governs just public accommodation. Finding somebody who knows what's going on and getting somebody who can guide you through the regulations will just make your life infinitely easier.

Having that edge will put your leaps and bounds ahead of the competition. When your establishment is more open and more welcoming, it's going to show up in the bottom line.

This also saves from the problem of thinking you don't have enough time to get started with business accessibility.

There are usually two big objections to doing anything about accessibility. I don't have time and I don't have money. I just can't afford to do it.

Most of the time it comes down to can you afford not to do it. When an award for an accessibility lawsuit is tens of thousands of dollars. And even if they don't prevail, you're talking about thousands of dollars in attorney fees, defending it and lost time on top of that. Can you afford not to do it?

Let's compare it to another piece of government regulation all of us are familiar with. How much time and money do businesses spend on complying with tax laws?

Every business owner hates it but they all do it if they want to stay in business. The cost of not doing it is simply too high.

There's a silver lining to complying with the ADA. There are ways to grease the rails and make things actually easier for you to do it.

Let's wipe the money issue off the table. Unlike tax compliance, the federal government incentivizes you to comply with the ADA.

The federal government will reimburse you up to $20,000 for doing accessible accessibility work. That includes the studies, includes consultation, includes engineering, and other things.

So, if you're saying, I can't afford that chunk out of my bottom line, you don't have to. Let's say you spend $10,000 this year and you turn around and, at the end of the year, you file your taxes and you get that $10,000 back. That's basically like spending no money. Yes, you have to put that money out there initially, but you get it back.

It gets better.

Let's just say you spent $20,000. It's deductible, but I can't deduct that whole $20,000 this year. You can actually take whatever you don't use and you apply it to the cost basis on the building and capitalize and depreciate it over the life of the building.

So, you come out ahead no matter what. The building instantly increases in value for tax purposes. And now for the cherry on top.

It's available every single year.

It's not just a one-time deal, it's an every single year deal. Until they change the tax laws, every single year there's 20,000 bucks that's sitting there that the federal government is willing to reimburse you for.

The federal government isn't the only one that does this. Some state governments do it. Some local governments. Even some provincial governments. I mean there's a lot of support to facilitate accessibility.

There are occasionally grants in certain areas. There's a lot of stuff that pops up. If you keep your eyes open, you can find money to pay for certain modifications.

If you're working with a consultant, they should know the amounts you would qualify for in your area. It's our job to keep track of the regulations and know what's out there in terms of tax credits and incentives.

While we may not be experts on every single place because every single place like to have their own little twist on things, we know where to look. When we come to an area and do any kind of accessibility work, one of the first things we do is find out what municipality they're in and so forth.

Then we can quickly research what things are available and can find out what tax incentives apply.

And it's in there to take advantage of. Why not use essentially free money to grow your business and make it more accessible?

Saving Time

Since we know that businesses need to devote time and money to accessibility and that there is a healthy chunk of money to help financially, we need to find ways to save time.

The easiest way to save time is to outsource the tasks associated with it. Get an expert, if you're not an expert yourself.

As a business owner, you need to wear enough hats every day in order to run and grow your business. If you're not an expert, it's okay to say, "I don't know". And the best way to save the time is to get a consultant and let them worry about accessibility. You keep worrying about running your business and they'll handle it.

Another way to save time is to talk to your customers and employees. If you're talking to your staff, there's a better than average chance that you have a staff member who has a disabled family member.

And if you're talking to your customers and you're asking them, what do you need? What can we do to make this a better experience for you? You will get answers.

And they're generally going to mention those things that are most important to them. If you poll your customers and ask, "Hey, is there anything we can do to improve the accessibility of this place?" They're going to know instantly because they live it.

So take advantage of every opportunity for instant feedback. You'll also save money this way because there are probably simple projects that can be done that will be seen as huge improvements.

We're a perfect example. We generally don't go to a couple different strip malls because parking lots are atrocious. The parking lots aren't maintained. The accessible parking isn't maintained. There are potholes, there's crap everywhere, and we just don't go.

The curb cuts aren't there. If you want to go to one store, you've got to go all the way down at the end. And then you'll find that the curb is gone. It's all broken away and you can't use the curb cut anyway.

So talk to people, they'll tell you what's going on. Start with the employees and customers, and then talk to organizations that deal with the disabled. Because people talk and they're going to be very, very willing to share the information.

It's not going to be like you're bothering them. You want the information and they want to share the information with you. That's why they're there. They want to help.

Biggest Mistake

The military has a saying, "Prior Planning Prevents Piss-Poor Performance". Business owners would do well to live by the same mantra.

Don't do projects before they're called for. What happens when you have plans to put an elevator in and you spent $10,000 making the bathroom accessible and the elevator shaft is going to go right where that bathroom is.

Now you're going have to wreck that out anyway, so that was a complete waste of your money. Planning prevents wasted money.

Get an engineer involved early in the process. involving an engineer from the get go is critical to making sure that your plan, when you put your plan together, involves less waste.

You're going to need an engineer for permitting because you'll need engineer drawings. It'll actually save you money in the long term because you're going to have somebody who's already familiar with your building, who already knows what you've been doing.

They'll also be aware of the progression of projects so they're able to plan structural changes ahead of time. This will set you up for that next step so that you don't wind up doing things that are going to have to wind up being torn out. There are some cases where that has to happen, but in a lot of cases that can be avoided.

Above all, don't believe in the "quick fixes". There are things that can be done more easily but, there's no panacea. Anyone you see peddling a cheap option is usually selling garbage.

Access Efficiency

The Americans with Disabilities Act has two parts to it. One was passed in the nineties and one was passed in 2010. There's permutations to things. You know, some things don't apply to anything built prior to 2012.

When have you known politicians to make anything easy for anybody? It's automatically overwhelming for a lot of people. You need an attorney to translate the stinking thing for you.

So, you need professionals who know the act as well as you possibly can and who are able to walk through a specific progress that is practical and makes sense to create access from the outside in and that it's integrated so that all your projects that are happening over whatever period of time are in support of one another and they're the most important thing to your employees and your customers.

You're overwhelmed from the get-go because you don't know what's required. You don't know what's right. The fear comes from not having the information you need at the start.

That's why we have courts, and even then, half the time, the attorneys get it wrong. By going through what we've discussed you'll alleviate the fear and overwhelm. Just move things forward.

Even if you did it entirely wrong, people are going to appreciate the fact that you are making the effort to be more accessible. But you can't please everybody either. You do your best to try to accommodate as many people as possible.

If you just get started, people are going to notice and talk about it. Don't be afraid to talk about it. Put it on your website. Hey, this is our accessibility plan. Our plan for the next three years is to completely upgrade the exterior parking areas and exterior of our stores to make them more accessible.

Come right out and ask for public feedback.

The reality of business is, if you're in business, you'll likely get sued sometime. When I was working as a contractor, I got sued several times. I know multiple guys who work in sales who have gotten sued several times.

There are certain people out there who are going to just sue. This drive-by lawsuit business is a cottage industry right now. Keep an eye out for people who say that they can stop all that because it's not possible.

But you can reduce a lot of it. Just by having a plan in place you're going to shorten the lifespan of a lot of these things by a large margin. Because simply by having a plan, you have proven that you are committed to removing barriers, which is what the law is actually about.

So what's our number one tip for being more efficient with business accessibility and getting better results with less effort?

The Practical Access methodology is inherently a more affordable, more efficient method of addressing accessibility. Because it's an outside in methodology. It's about getting people into the building and then addressing the things inside the building that need to be addressed as they need to be addressed in a common sense fashion.

It's automatically more efficient, and you're dealing with customer accessibility, staff accessibility, all those things at the same time as opposed to the scattershot approach.

Our Revelations

One of Dawn's biggest 'aha' moments as a disabled individual was realizing that not all accessibility is practical. There was a restaurant in Florida that she was in, and the staff was wonderful. They were so excited because they had an upper level and they had a lift.

They installed the lift to go up about three stairs that you roll onto the lift and it lifts you up. And they were so excited to get to use it because they had spent money to get it in there.

Okay. She went up the lift, rolled off, and the tables were so crowded up on that level, she couldn't turn around. That was definitely an 'aha' moment that, Okay, we're not creating practical accessibility.

She didn't even think of it in those terms back then, but the 'aha' moment was, not all accessibility is necessary, good or not.

All of it helps. "We've got the second level and we want people to be able to get to it." If you can create accessible spaces in a more convenient location, they don't give a crap whether you have a lift or not.

But it was so good that they were so excited. "We spent the money to do this, we finally get to use it. We want this person to be able to go up on the second level!" Yeah, I'm up here now. What do I do?

It's not just from a customer standpoint either. Dawn has been an employee in several places where, even in a supervisory position, where you are dealing with things like this.

She had a job where she had to buy her own furniture because they didn't have the furniture to accommodate her and they didn't even know where to get it. So she just bought her own.

Frank's moment came from an emergency call from a panicked store owner. He had a franchise in a leased building and had gotten fined. Frank did some research and made a surprising discovery.

If you're leasing a building and you don't own the building, you're still partly responsible for the accessibility of your store. No matter who the building owner is.

That's not to say the building owner has no responsibility. But it's kind of a shared thing. And a lot of these places are triple net leases anymore where the tenant is responsible for maintenance and responsible for a lot of things.

So, building owners are kind of trying to pass the buck, but building owners still have some culpability when it comes to accessibility. So it's a shared responsibility and just because you're leasing a building does not mean you're not responsible for the accessibility.

Into the Future

With more and more disabled people going out into the community and wanting to do things the requirements are just going to expand. This isn't going away. It's just going to increase.

In the seventies and eighties when we were kids, you didn't see as much of the people in wheelchairs and all that stuff. It was just getting started.

Frank can actually remember when they first put a wheelchair ramp on his junior high school. It was this monstrosity that cost some exorbitant amount of money that was outside.

This is Pennsylvania and school was happening most of the time in the wintertime. So it wasn't even usable for most of the school year.

These days the technology has come a long way. Vehicles can accommodate more types of disabilities than ever. More people are able to drive, frighteningly enough in some cases. You can drive a vehicle with a joystick now.

Frank met a man with Cerebral Palsy who had a van that he drove with a joystick. Just the thought caused a few nightmares.

So they're able to drive. That means they're able to get to stores. That means they're able to start using public accommodations. And as technology improves, you're going to start to see more and more and more. And people are going to demand a higher level of accessibility simply because of the fact that so many people are now out there and utilizing services.

Do you want to miss out on them as customers or clients being able to serve them, being able to have them come into your business?

Dawn's inner accountant can't help referring to the bottom line. That you are in business to make revenues, and if you don't, you don't have a business. So do you want to miss out on this? There's so much potential here and it's easy to get started. So it's, it's a win-win.

Not to go too far off track, but as an example, we have a convenience store. And they are rebuilding their stores all over the place. When they first started, I figured they were just going to give them a face lift.

You cannot imagine when I first walked into one of the newly remodeled stores! They have excellent accessible parking and then straight path to the door. There is a small vestibule for HVAC energy savings, but a button opens both doors.

You go in and the aisles are super wide. The shelves are not as tall so everything is easily reached. There is always extra staff members there and if, if you were to need help, they've always got somebody there to help you.

There's also a button on the gas pumps so you can call somebody out, they'll come out, and pump your gas.

So it's unbelievable how fantastic an experience it is. As a regular able-bodied customer going in there, it's just more open and more inviting and just a better environment altogether.

And knowing that Dawn could go in there, that if she drove down to this convenience store and went in, that she could go in and get her own stuff with zero trouble. That's an amazing thing.

And this is a convenience store. So if a convenience store can do it, any business can do it.

We have a local conservancy here. It's just getting started with some things and they're doing some projects and a lot of those things are happening through the Boy Scouts.

One of the things that they did right out of the gate is provide a pathway. It's not perfect, and they had their hiccups with execution, but it provided a pathway so that this girl (Dawn) who grew up in the country, who hadn't been in the woods in years since she was 18, was finally able to actually go out and enjoy going into the woods again.

The path is power, wheelchair accessible, not manual, but still, being in a power chair and just being able to go by herself was incredible.

They're being proactive about It. They're just getting started and they already have spent the money to provide a pathway for mobility-impaired people to enjoy nature.

Their other efforts are kind of in conjunction with that pathway. They're working off of that pathway and going outwards and they already have plans to expand their pathways to reach more areas as they're added.

That's an example of the proper plan. They're way ahead of the curve as far as accessibility is concerned.

Whereas you see a lot of the federal and state parks that are now trying to get things to be more accessible. For instance, our Boy Scout camp did a lot of stuff to try to make things more accessible.

There's a lot of money involved to retroactively do it. And doing it retroactively actually starts to create other problems that then need to be solved.

These are two examples where an organization has made accessibility a priority. In the case of the conservancy, they could honestly with complete validity say, "Hey, there's no money in the budget for this. We operate on donations" But they went the extra mile to provide something where now you see elderly people up there and they are able to walk in it shaded in areas and stuff like that.

It's a really good example of proactive, practical planning. This the direction everyone is going to have to go to stay competitive.

Final Thoughts

Practical Access is intended to be a more holistic, integrated system. We tried to create a method that is more natural and makes sense.

We wanted to be thoughtful about what makes sense to do and when, and creating a process by which a business owner knows what needs to happen next, while still meeting all the requirements,

The makes the development of a plan less onerous because the progression just kind of makes sense. As in, "Can somebody get to this accommodation that I am actually thinking about doing?" If no, then you don't do it yet. You do something that gets them to that point.

If the answer to "Can somebody use this right away?" is no, then step back and address the thing that allows them to be able to get to that point.

It addresses customers and staff at the same time so that it's not a lopsided operation. It improves your company culture overall because it makes your staff feel as valued as the customers.

It lets everyone know that you care about everybody, you care about your customers, you care about your staff. Their wellbeing and their happiness is important to you and their ability to enjoy your facility.

Whether it's an office building, a store, or something else entirely. We talk a lot about retail environments simply because that seems to be one of the places that people see the most.

And offices are actually starting to become less used but that could change. Any facility owner should be addressing accessibility.

We want to reinforce how important it is to get started. Do it now. The requirements are not going away. They're probably only going to expand.

This is something that needs to happen sooner rather than later. It's not something to be afraid of. It's not big and scary. There are people that can help you. They can put you on the right path to doing this and guide you.

There are ways to mitigate the expenses in both time and money and it's way worth it. Just the good will that you are generating by being proactive is priceless.

Then the actual genuine ROI on every single dollar spent is going to be a hundred x or more. Because you're creating an entire feeling of community around your brand. You're actually demonstrating that you're an inclusive community brand that cares about its staff and its customers that's going to pay dividends.

And don't think that you're just talking about stock people and clerks and stuff like that. I mean, Dawn is a CFO in a wheelchair. So from bottom to top is accessibility. You need to be addressing it throughout your organization so that people like her are accommodated.

You're also talking about C-suite individuals and you're talking about middle managers. You're talking about people at every level of your organization that will make use of those, those accommodations. You'll gain some unexpected top talent.

Finally, you can't ignore how all this is going to positively affect you personally. Simply doing good is sometimes its own reward.

Yeagers Consulting

We offer many services to businesses to enable them to get the maximum value from their properties. We offer training to help facility owners evaluate and handle their own accessibility. Done With You training and services are available or you can have us handle it all. There is also training available to owners, executives, and other staff for interacting with disabled people.

Helping businesses provide better customer service to all their potential customers is our passion. When you hire us, you're getting people who understand the built environment as well as living with a disability.

We know what to look for and what actually works and what isn't worth it. We also have the educational and professional background to know how the use of your property affects the bottom line of a business and how it affects the culture of an industry as well.

If you have any questions about Practical Access or other services that we offer, you can learn more or contact us at yeagersconsulting.com.

We hope that you have found this information useful and that it enables you to take your accessibility efforts to the next level.

www.ingramcontent.com/pod-product-compliance
Lightning Source LLC
Chambersburg PA
CBHW050309220526
45465CB00005B/1923